A Bird Is a Bird

Lizzy Rockwell

SONG
SPARROW

Holiday House / New York

For Ken

The publisher thanks Stephen C. Quinn, Exhibition Associate at the
American Museum of Natural History, and Dr. Alexandra M. Class Freeman,
Art Editor of the *Handbook of Bird Biology*, Cornell Lab of Ornithology,
for reviewing this book.

Printed and Bound in October 2014 at Tien Wah Press, Johor Bahru, Johor, Malaysia.
The artwork was created with gouache, watercolor, and colored pencil on Fabriano hot press watercolor paper.
www.holidayhouse.com
First Edition
1 3 5 7 9 10 8 6 4 2
Library of Congress Cataloging-in-Publication Data
Rockwell, Lizzy.
A bird is a bird / by Lizzy Rockwell. — First edition.
pages cm
ISBN 978-0-8234-3042-0 (hardcover)
1. Birds—Juvenile literature. I. Title.
QL676.2.R632 2015
598—dc23
2013018289

COMMON
OSTRICH
(FEMALE)

COMMON
OSTRICH
(MALE)

A bird may be tall.

COMMON
OSTRICH
(MALE)

A bird may be small.

SUPERB
STARLING

One bird is fancy.

DUTCH BANTAM
ROOSTER
(MALE)

Another is plain.
But a bird is a bird.
A bird is a bird because . . .

WHITE
LEGHORN
CHICKEN
(FEMALE)

a bird has a beak.

TOCO TOUCAN

A beak helps a
bird pick fruit.

SCARLET
MACAW

BLUE-HEADED
PARROT

9

WOOD STORK

BROWN PELICAN

WHITE
IBIS

GREAT EGRET

GREEN HERON

A beak catches fish.

GREAT BLUE
HERON

ROSEATE
SPOONBILL

PILEATED
WOODPECKER
(MALE)

A beak can peck.

A beak
can get
to nectar.

RUBY-THROATED
HUMMINGBIRD
(MALE)

A bird is a bird because . . .

ANDEAN
CONDOR
(MALE)

a bird has two wings.
Wings flap and glide.

Wings help swim and dive.

KING PENGUINS

A bird is a bird because . . .

a bird starts out in an egg.

AMERICAN
ROBIN

An egg can be
in a nest in a tree.

An egg can be
in a nest on the ground.

SPOTTED SANDPIPER

But wait!

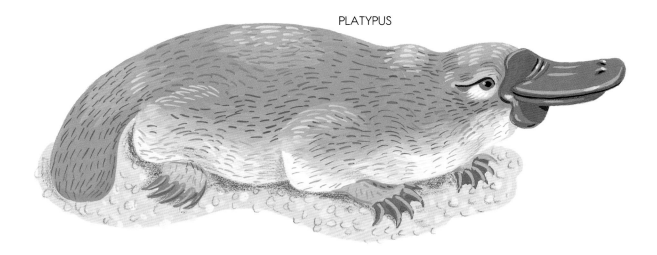

PLATYPUS

A platypus has a beak.

HOUSEFLY

A fly has wings.

And a snake starts out in an egg.
Are they birds too?

NEW MEXICO
MILK SNAKE

No, only a bird is a bird.
Because only a bird has . . .

feathers!

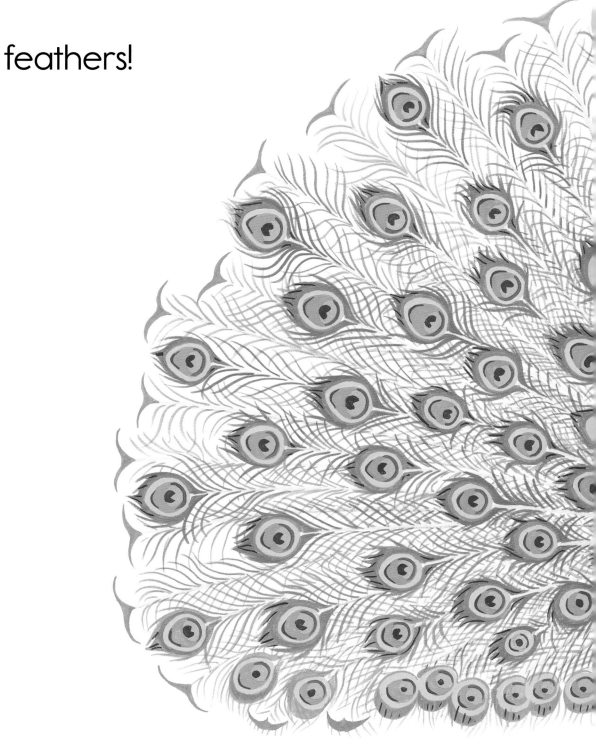

INDIAN PEAFOWL
(MALE PEACOCK)

Feathers can stand out.

BROWN
CREEPER

Feathers can blend in.

WHIP-POOR-WILL

EASTERN
SCREECH
OWL

HERRING GULL

RED-BREASTED MERGANSER (MALE)

MALLARD
(FEMALE)

Feathers help birds fly. Feathers help birds stay warm and dry.

CANADA GOOSE

MALLARD
(MALE)

BUFFLEHEAD
(MALE)

BUFFLEHEAD
(FEMALE)

AMERICAN
GOLDFINCH
(MALE)

SAFFRON
FINCH
(MALE)

CARDINAL (MALE)

AMERICAN
FLAMINGO

KING BIRD-
OF-PARADISE
(MALE)

SCARLET IBIS

SULFUR-CRESTED
COCKATOO

Feathers of every color

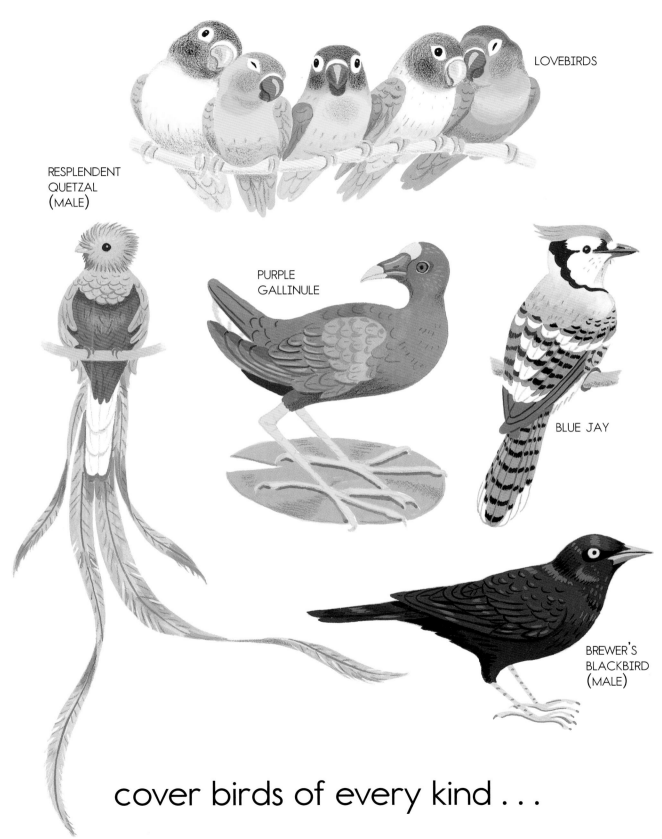

LOVEBIRDS

RESPLENDENT
QUETZAL
(MALE)

PURPLE
GALLINULE

BLUE JAY

BREWER'S
BLACKBIRD
(MALE)

cover birds of every kind . . .

ROCK PIGEON

because only a bird is a bird.